NATIONAL GEOGRAPHIC

T0040384

It's Dinner Time

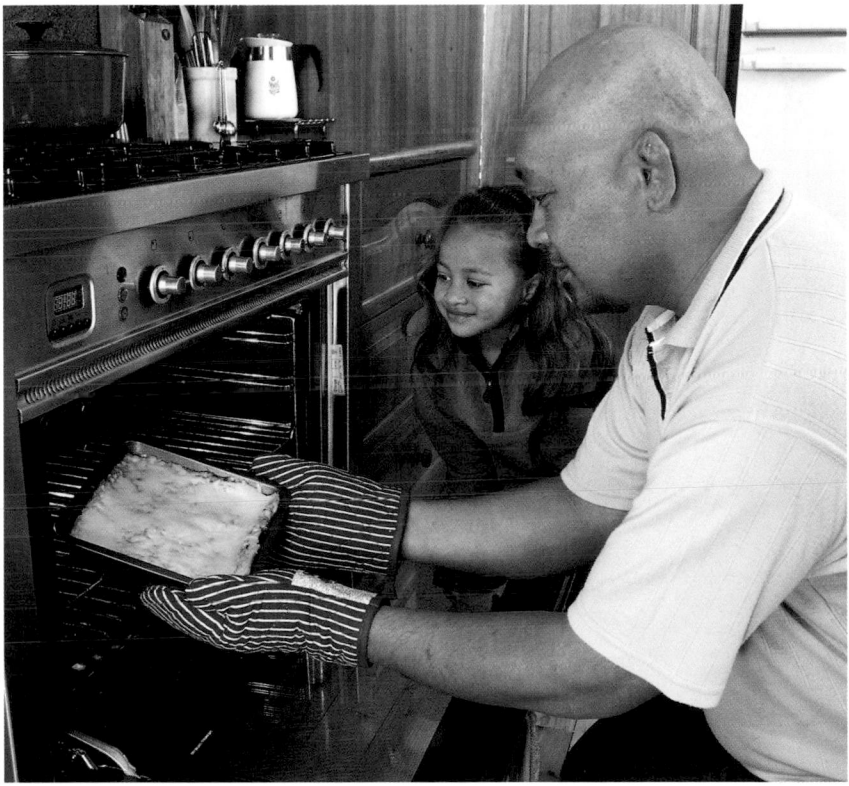

Ming Tan

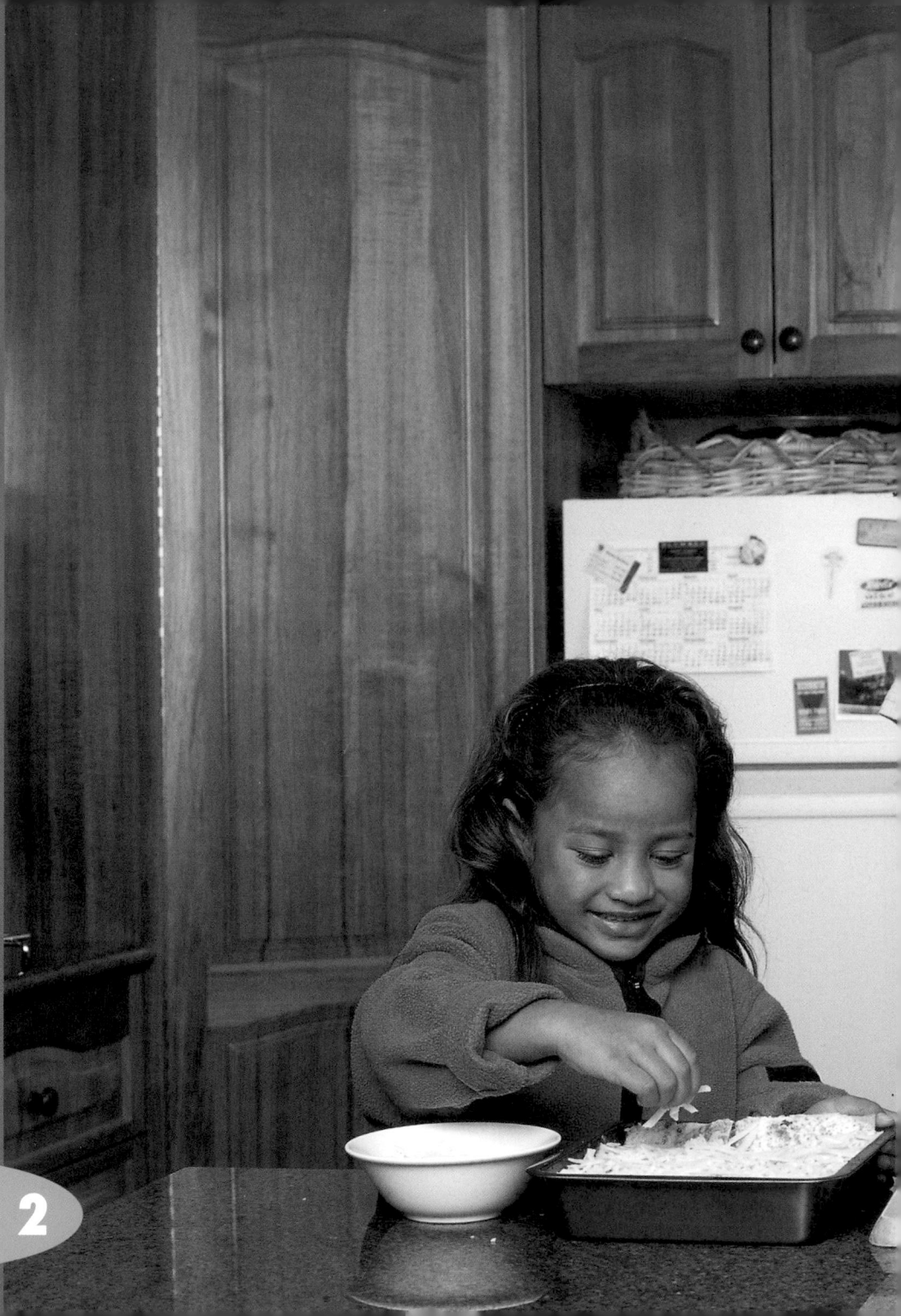

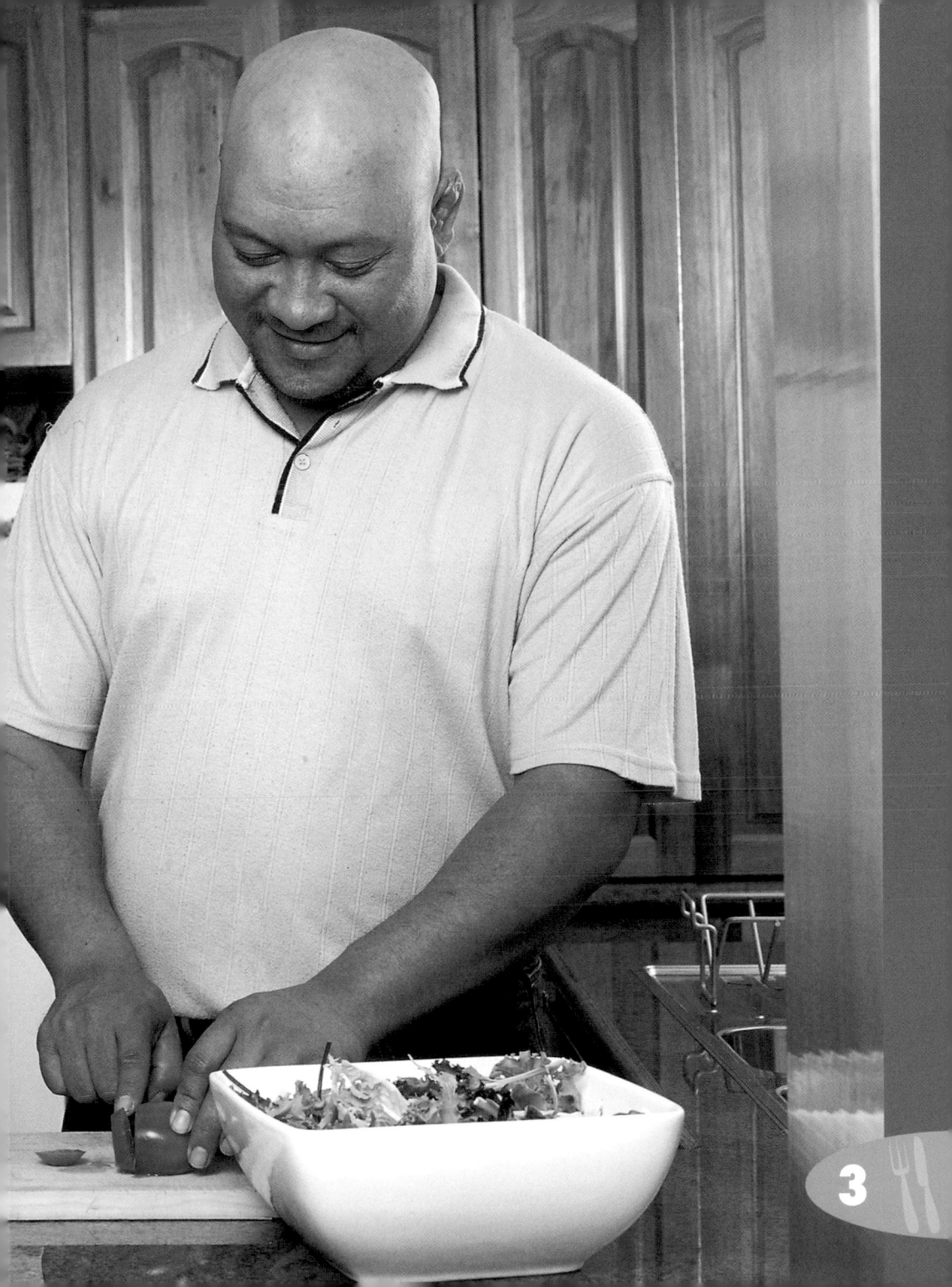

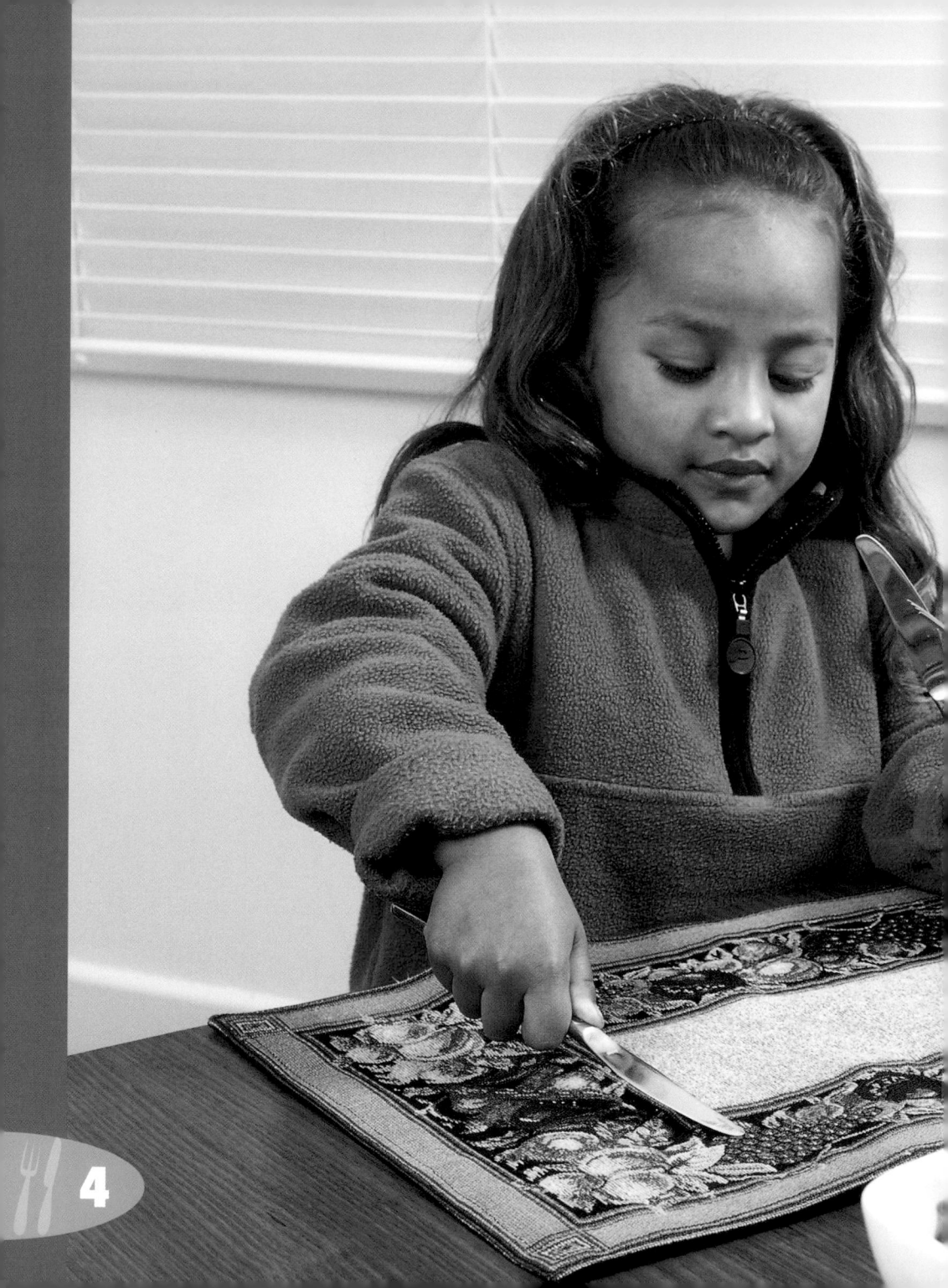

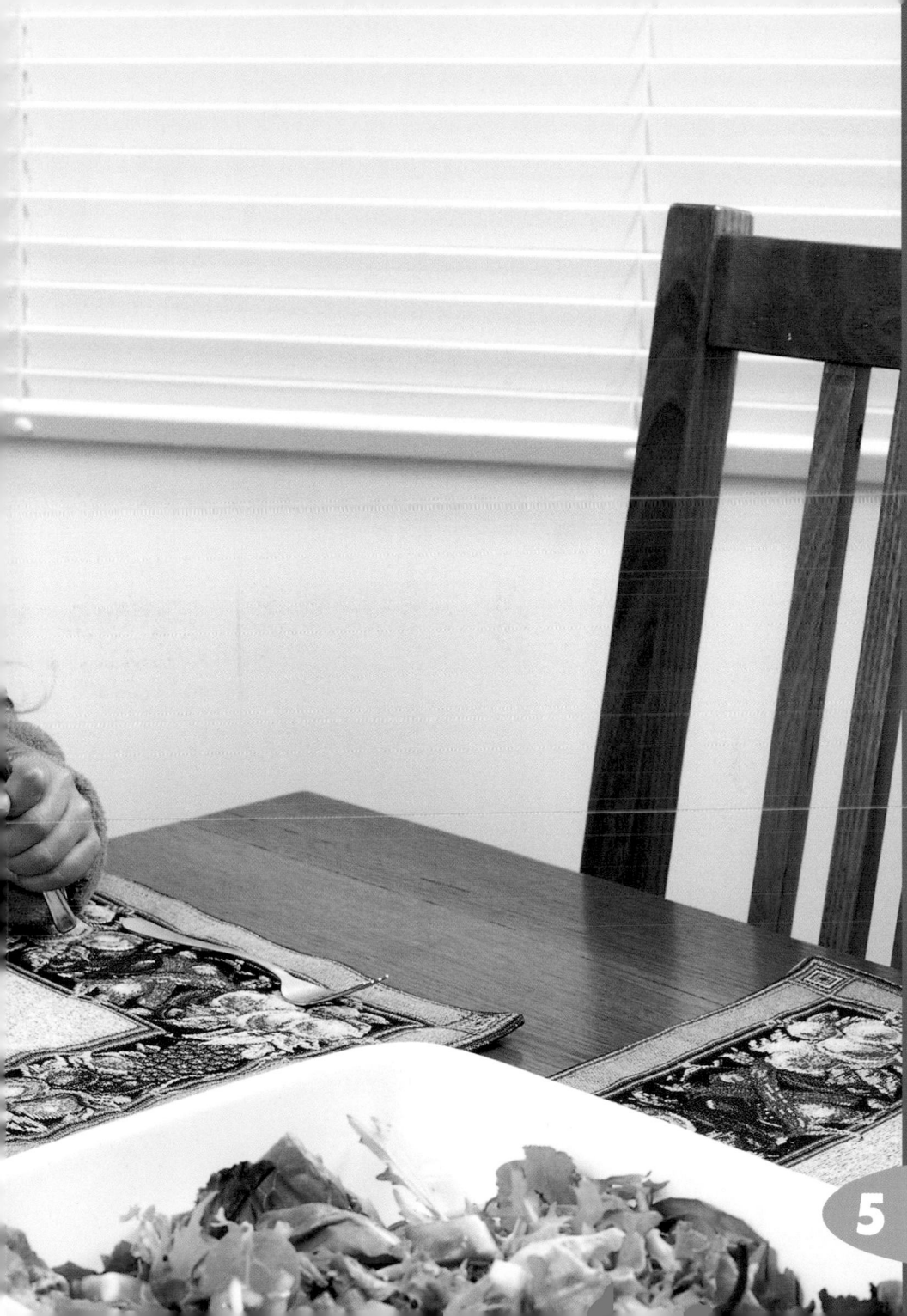

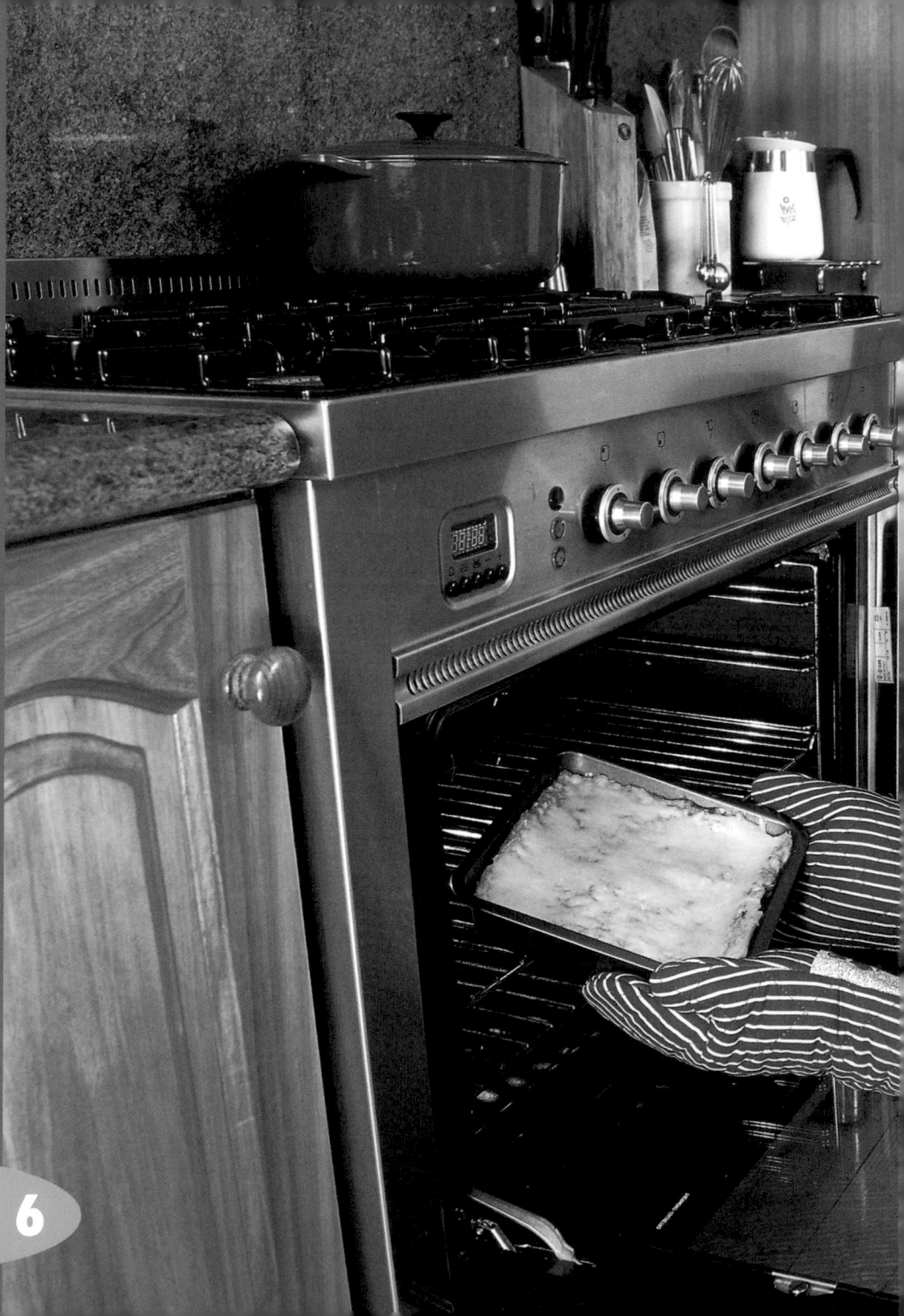

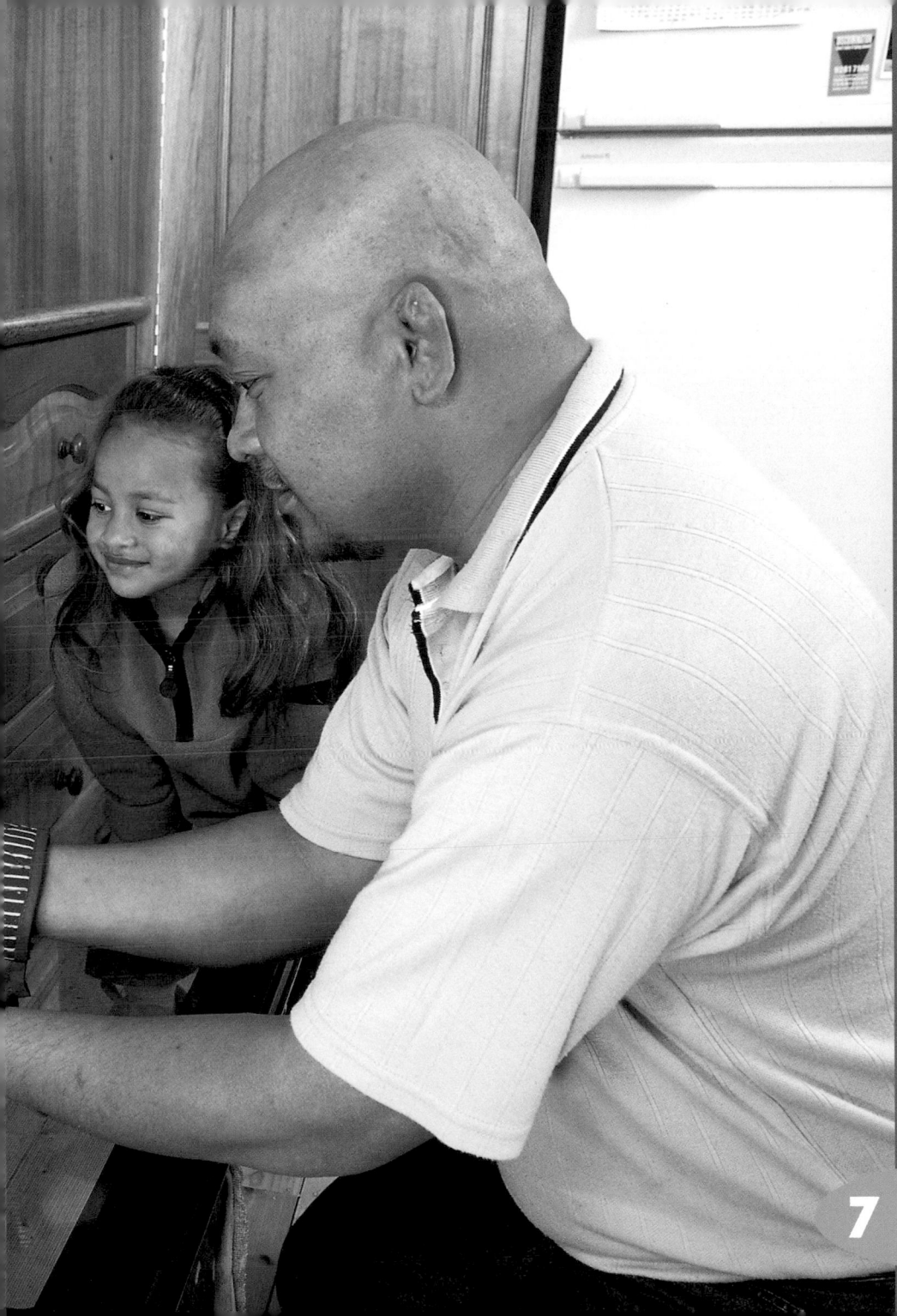

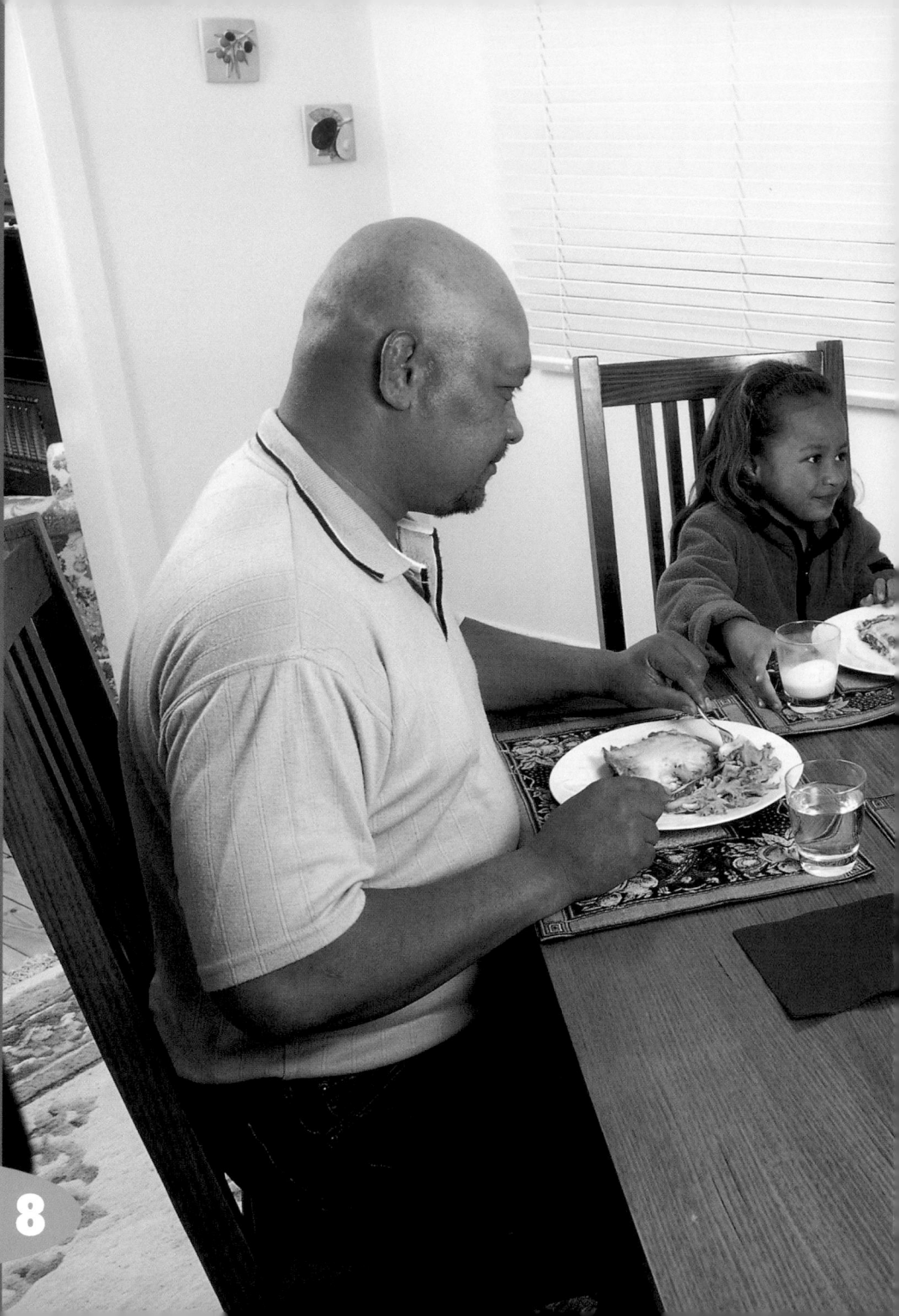

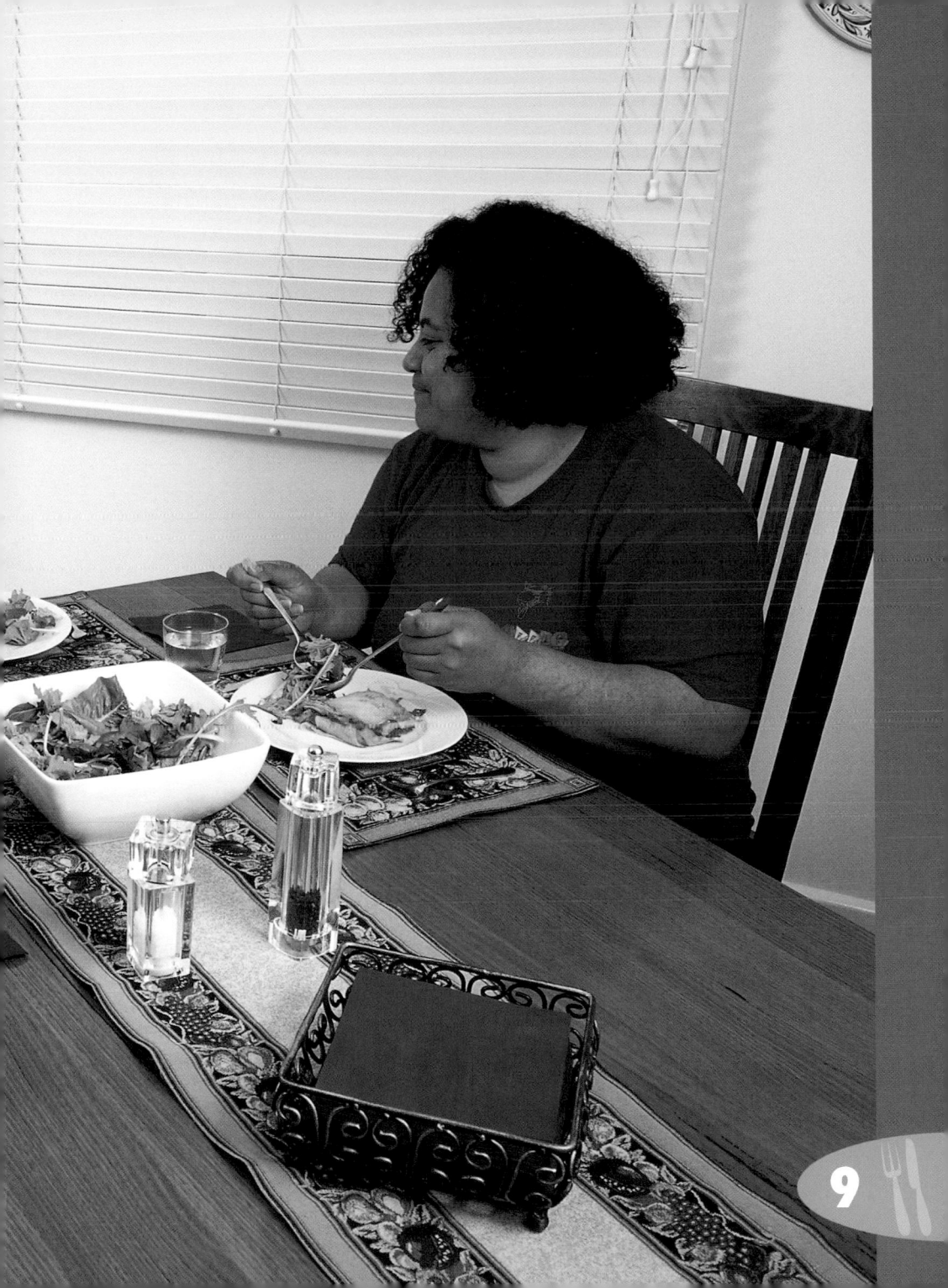

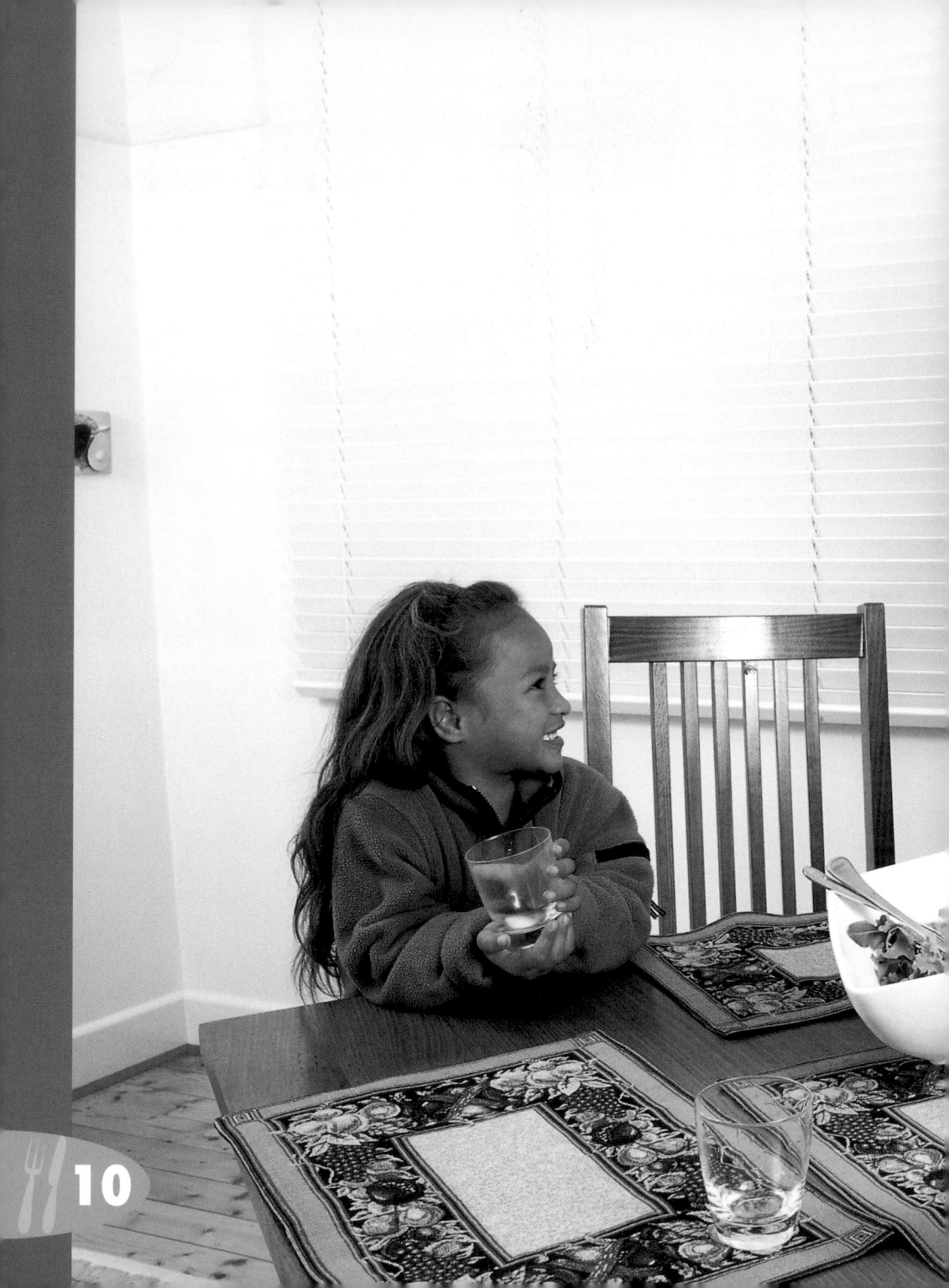

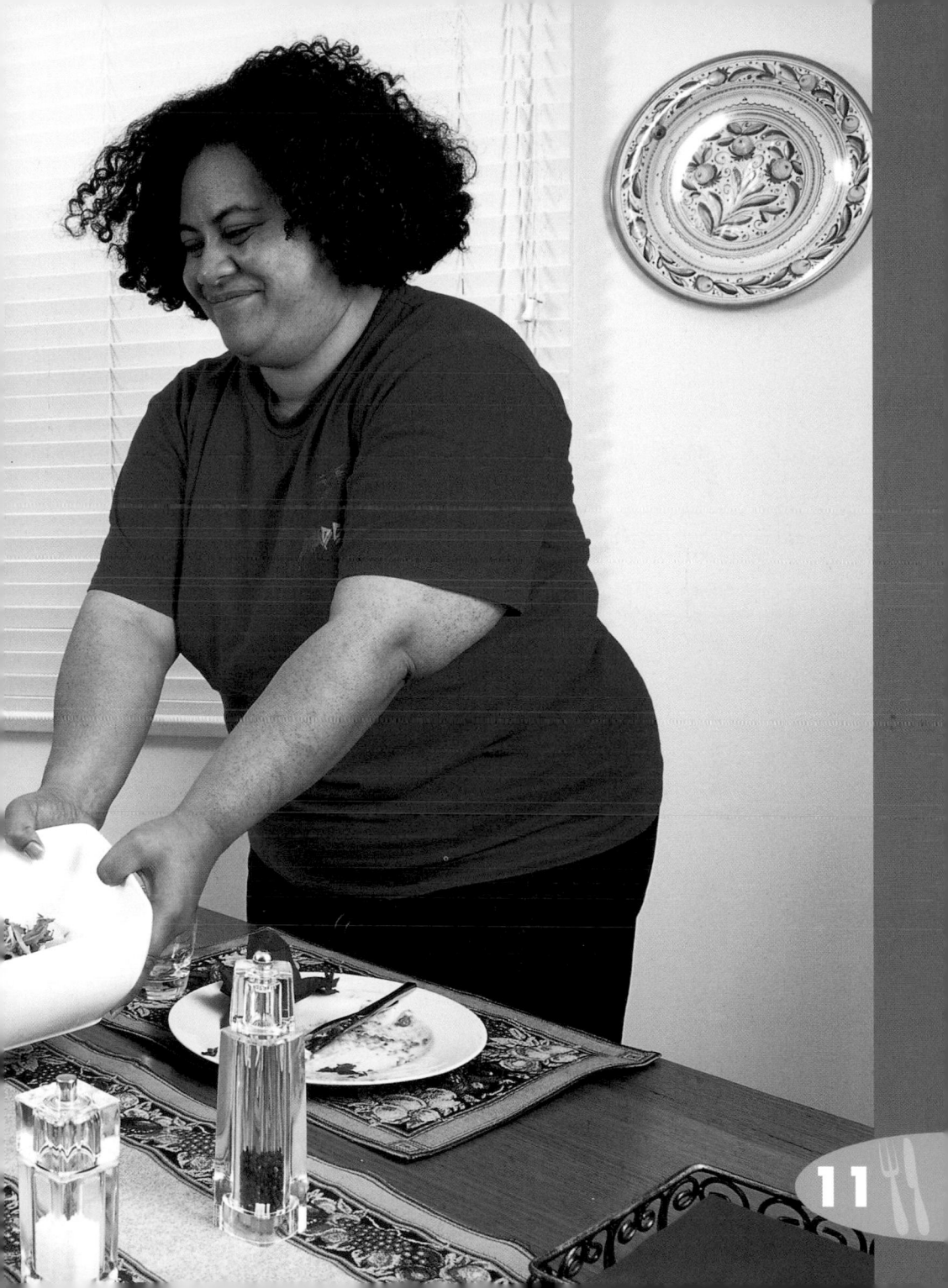

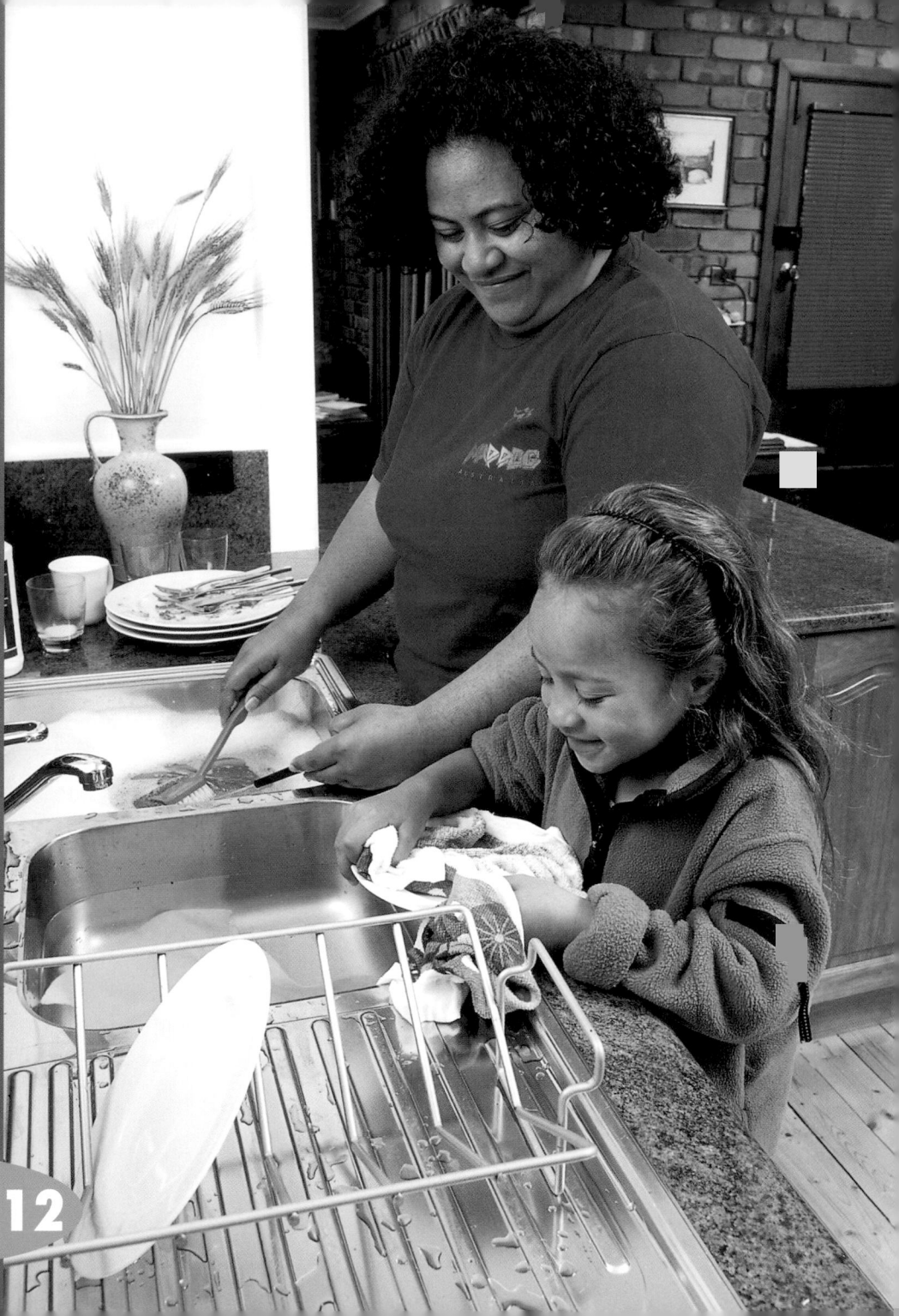